THE REVELATION

The Revelation
30 Rules of Effectiveness

Kris M. Drake, FACHE

Page Publishing
New York

Copyright © 2019 Kris M. Drake, FACHE
All rights reserved
First Edition

PAGE PUBLISHING, INC.
Conneaut Lake, PA

First originally published by Page Publishing 2019

ISBN 978-1-64544-257-8 (pbk)
ISBN 978-1-64544-258-5 (digital)

Printed in the United States of America

CONTENTS

Acknowledgments ix

Rule I:	Self-Assessment 3
Rule II:	Pinpoint Your Niche 4
Rule III:	Targeted Networking 5
Rule IV:	Honor Your Network 6
Rule V:	Preparation is Essential 7
Rule VI:	Interview Day Strategy 8
Rule VII:	Premium Level Post-Interview Follow Up 9
Rule VIII:	Solid References 10
Rule IX:	Responding to the Phone Call 11
Rule X:	The Offer Arrives 12
Rule XI:	Securing an Attorney 13
Rule XII:	Finalizing Negotiations in Writing 14
Rule XIII:	Notifying Your Employer 15
Rule XIV:	Immediate Priorities 19
Rule XV:	Mid-term Priorities 20
Rule XVI:	Mind Your Nutrition 21

Rule XVII:	The Curtain Call	22
Rule XVIII:	Calm Your Mind	23
Rule XIX:	Be a Positivity Champion	24
Rule XX:	Listening Is Not Enough	25
Rule XXI:	Avoid Professional Suicide	26
Rule XXII:	How to Navigate Organizational Events	27
Rule XXIII:	Team Centeredness	28
Rule XXIV:	Stay Steady	29
Rule XXV:	Purpose-driven Meetings	30
Rule XXVI:	Solve the Tough Problems	31
Rule XXVII:	Use "Other Duties as Assigned" to Your Professional Advantage	32
Rule XXVIII:	Embrace Your Mistakes	33
Rule XXIX:	Over-appreciate Your Executive/Administrative Assistants	34
Rule XXX:	Encourage Solutions	35

Closing Remarks 37

Appendices 39

About the Author 50

ACKNOWLEDGMENTS

I would like to take this opportunity to dedicate this book to people who were very influential in my personal and professional life. My mother, grandmother, and father placed heavy emphasis on academic achievement and spiritual actualization. If it were not for their constant encouragement throughout the years, this work would not have been possible. My long-time mentor, Brad Mathis, has been a stable in my professional journey for the past decade. I would like to thank him for his wisdom, honest feedback, and courage to always tell me what I needed to hear. My brothers Ladon and Willie and sister Priscilla have been there for me throughout my entire life, leading by example. I would like to thank them for lending an ear during my times of struggle, encouraging me to maintain a strong relationship with God, and showing me what brotherly and sisterly love truly means. I would like to thank my childhood friend Brett for standing by my side for so many years. His words of encouragement and overall support are beyond measure.

Lastly, I would like to dedicate this book to my brother Deion, my nephews and nieces, most notably Arielle. Throughout the years, I have tried to lead by example, pass along wisdom and be there for you at every opportunity. My hope is that this book inspires you to shoot for the stars and lead lives that bring the highest honor to God, our family, and mankind.

The Revelation

SECTION 1

Searching for the Right Job

Let's face it. Job hunting can be a very daunting task. In all ways, job hunting is a job in and of itself. The set of rules that follows include key principles for effectively landing a job. While nothing is 100 percent effective, these rules are tried and true methods that create leads, interviews, job offers, and the employment agreement that you desire.

RULE I

Self-Assessment

Before you start your job search, it is important to do a fair assessment of your knowledge, skills, abilities, and experiences. The reason for doing this exercise is to clarify what's in scope, and out of scope, relative to your abilities and next job. This gap analysis can also identify areas that need strengthening before beginning your job search. I would highly encourage you to seek out the assistance of a career coach or close friend who is very skilled at this sort of activity. The end product of this exercise is an updated résumé and a compelling leadership value proposition.

RULE 11

Pinpoint Your Niche

Once you have taken stock of your skills/abilities and addressed any gaps, you need to determine what type of work you are interested in doing. For example, are you interested in a job that is slow paced and predicable, or something more fast paced and ever changing? Are you interested in working from home? Do you like the idea of getting up and driving to work every day? Are you seeking full-time or part-time work? Are you interested in work that is task-oriented, or work that requires more critical thinking and decision-making? Your responses to these questions will better define what type of work you are looking for.

RULE III

Targeted Networking

Once you have updated your résumé, clarified both your leadership value proposition and type of work you are interested in, it is now time to inform your network of your intentions. You can approach this in numerous ways. Some options include inviting your friends for lunch, coffee or tea, or dinner. Regardless of which option you select, given that you are the initiator, you should cover the tab. This is a very considerate and appropriate gesture on your part and an act of good will.

During your networking meeting, please resist the temptation of being shy at all cost! Tell your friends what you are interested in doing and solicit their advice. Your friends may have access to critical information such as upcoming conferences related to your line of work, list serves with job openings, industry-leading headhunters or search firms, contacts at certain organizations, and possibly job vacancies at their place of employment. If you play your cards right, you might end your day with promising leads, key contacts, an introduction to an organization, and possibly an interview. One more thing—do not forget to ask for your friends to circulate your résumé! This is good practice.

RULE IV

Honor Your Network

Because networking is the most effective way for landing jobs, we will explore this pathway more fully. Your network friends have gone to bat for you. Avoid making them look bad at all cost. This means that you put forth your A-game in all encounters. Remember, your friends' reputations are on the line. Again, do not let them down! If the shoe was on the other foot, you would have equal or higher expectations of them.

RULE V

Preparation is Essential

You have tapped your network for leads and landed an on-site interview. However, your job has just begun. At this stage, you need to make sure that you are well prepared to answer behavioral based questions in the STAR (situation, task, action, result) format. Further, learn everything you can about the company, including mission, vision, values, history, financial performance, competitors, and relevant market share information. Lastly, if possible, study up on your interviewer(s).

RULE VI

Interview Day Strategy

On interview day, when you arrive, greet everyone you encounter at the organization with a smile and handshake. During interviews, knowledge and flattery can carry your candidacy a very long way. And remember, the interview is a conversation, so be prepared to answer and ask very meaningful questions. Before interview day concludes, ask the hiring manager about the next steps of the process and reiterate your interest in the vacant position. And as a simple reminder, please ask each interviewer for his/her business card. You will need this information for follow up purposes.

RULE VII

Premium Level Post-Interview Follow Up

Post-interview follow-up is an opportunity to distinguish yourself as a standout candidate. As a rule of thumb, you should follow up with a thank-you note between twenty-four and seventy-two hours after the interview. The manner to which you follow up with the prospective employer is vital. While many professionals type up thank-you letters, I highly advise against this approach. Instead, I recommend that you produce and submit handwritten thank-you notes to each of your interviewers, including executive assistants that you met on interview day. If you are worried about timeliness, the post office offers express options that ship and deliver thank-you notes overnight. **(See the sample thank-you note in the appendix section.)**

RULE VIII

Solid References

Your prospective employer will complete a background and reference check. As good practice, you need to make sure that your professional references are solid. Three professional references are more than adequate. After all, at this stage of the process, you do not want anything to put your candidacy in jeopardy.

RULE IX

Responding to the Phone Call

Congratulations! You just received a phone call from a prospective employer with news of their interest in extending a job offer to you. How do you respond? You express gratitude for their selection, reiterate your excitement about joining the team, and express your interest in working with them to finalize a job offer that works for both parties. The job offer will come to you in the form of an employment agreement. In terms of next steps, you can expect to receive an employment agreement from the prospective employer in e-mail or paper format.

RULE X

The Offer Arrives

Upon receipt of the initial job offer or employment agreement, you should consult with your attorney. If you do not have an attorney, you should secure an attorney, who specializes in employment law, right away. Before you meet with your attorney, you need to have a strong sense of what you are willing to accept or not accept (i.e. non-negotiables) in an employment agreement. Review the agreement, write up your questions, and schedule an appointment with your attorney. Your attorney will go over the employment agreement in its entirety with you paragraph by paragraph to ensure your understanding of the offer.

RULE XI

Securing an Attorney

Once you meet with your attorney to discuss the employment agreement and your needs, it is time to present a counteroffer to the prospective employer. You will need to submit your counteroffer in written format. The counteroffer letter needs to strike a conciliatory tone yet articulate your needs as a future employee. Upon receipt of the counteroffer letter, the prospective employer will likely suggest a phone call to address your requests. Again, before you speak with the prospective employer, jot down your list of questions and must-haves. If you opt for your attorney to negotiate on your behalf, provide him or her with your list of must-haves and non-negotiables. **(See the sample counteroffer letter in the appendix section.)**

RULE XII

Finalizing Negotiations in Writing

If the prospective employer agrees to all or most of your terms, make sure that you get the final employment agreement in writing. Once you have a finalized, signed written employment agreement in hand, the last detail is to finalize your start date with the employer. Once your start date has been finalized, you have officially completed the hiring process. Congratulations on landing your new job!

RULE XIII

Notifying Your Employer

You have landed a new job offer. How do you go about notifying your current employer? As a professional courtesy, you should provide your current employer with at least a thirty- to sixty-day notification of your resignation. This is more than ample time for the current employer to develop a transition plan, identify an interim person, and wrap up any projects for which you were responsible.

SECTION 2

Being Effective on the Job

You have started your new job with high levels of energy and excitement. You want to make a good first and lasting impression. The next set of rules include key tips on being effective in your new job. While the list is not exhaustive, practicing these rules will put you in position to be very effective and highly influential as a new or tenured employee.

RULE XIV

Immediate Priorities

In your first meeting with your supervisor, clarify your objectives for the next thirty, sixty, ninety days. Once your supervisor has clarified your short-term objectives, focus on both learning the organization's culture and completing those objectives. You want to demonstrate exemplary performance in the first ninety days on the job.

RULE XV

Mid-term Priorities

Once you have completed your short-term objectives, make sure that you meet with your supervisor and clarify your midterm objectives for the next six to nine months. Once your supervisor has clarified your objectives, focus your energy on completing these objectives. If something new emerges, speak with your supervisor about the new initiative and clarify if new initiatives fall within or outside of your objectives. Again, you want to demonstrate exemplary performance in the first year on the job.

RULE XVI

Mind Your Nutrition

Never go to work on an empty stomach. You need vitamins and minerals to energize your mind and body. Without a balanced and nutritious meal, you will not possess the energy to lead. As a result, your leadership productivity will suffer due to fatigue and lack of focus.

RULE XVII

The Curtain Call

I firmly believe that success begins and ends in the mind. As Benjamin Franklin once said, "You can achieve whatever you put your mind to." However, the work does not stop there. Not even close! Using Hollywood phraseology, "You need to think the part and look the part before you can play the part." In the professional world, appearance matters. What's more, first impressions are lasting impressions. Therefore, if you seek to be successful, you need to think, speak, and dress like a professional every day and in every way. Take this advice to heart!

RULE XVIII

Calm Your Mind

Meditate or pray before you start your day. The intent is to calm your mind and find your focus. Without a center of focus, you run the risk of delivering a less than optimal leadership product. If you are not able to pray or meditate, there are other alternatives for achieving calm and focus such as herbal tea. Regardless of your method, calm your mind and find your focus at the beginning of each day.

RULE XIX

Be a Positivity Champion

Start every morning on a positive note. Focus on little gestures and communications, such as a friendly handshake and/or "good morning." The intent is to set your personal expectations very high and allow them to carry the day. If done properly, your positive energy will influence the environment and everyone with which you interact.

RULE XX

Listening Is Not Enough

In all likelihood, you have read this phrase before—be an active listener. This is great advice. However, I would like to rephrase and redirect. My experiences suggest that you not only need to be an active listener—you need to be consistently invested in the other person's development. This requires the skill of patience and understanding. Remember, this is not about you—it is about the example you set through your behavior.

RULE XXI

Avoid Professional Suicide

Throughout your professional journey, you will come across people (men and women) who push an organization's cultural boundaries. They can appear in any form—an early careerist with a chip on his or her shoulder or a supposedly seasoned leader with tenure and significant levels of influence. Regardless of their career status, at a timing and place of their choosing, they may decide to "let their hair down" and exhibit conduct that is in clear violation of the organization's core values and guiding behaviors. If you encounter these individuals, do not engage! It is situationally risky, politically unwise, and quite frankly, professional suicide.

RULE XXII

How to Navigate Organizational Events

At some point, you will be invited to an event, party, or some sort of gathering organized by your company, supervisor, colleague, or someone affiliated to your workplace. Please approach these invitations with extreme caution. Remember, your professional reputation is not confined to your office. On the contrary, your reputation follows you into the broader community, and the lights and cameras are always fixed upon you. If you decide to attend an organizational event, I encourage you to consider two things. First, refrain from consuming any alcoholic beverage of any sort. You want to appear sharp at all times, and an overindulgence in alcohol shows lack of control. Secondly, consider arriving early and leaving early. My personal preference to organizational events is to attend for the first forty-five minutes and consume no alcohol. Lastly, do not forget to mingle!

RULE XXIII

Team Centeredness

In a leadership position, you are expected to support your team and set them up for success. To this end, focus less on you and more on your team's success. Make sure that you give them to tools and support to be successful. If they win, you win. It is really that simple.

RULE XXIV

Stay Steady

In day-to-day organizational affairs, you are faced with numerous challenges and decisions. If you do not prioritize appropriately, you will find yourself in a state of mental paralysis without a pathway forward. To prevent this from happening, you, as a leader, need to know what matters. This is where you dedicate your time and energy. Whenever you feel unclear about the organization's direction, you should meet with your supervisor and clarify what matters for the time frame of interest (month, quarter, year, etc.). Otherwise, you are at risk of drifting from organizational objectives and moving toward ineffectiveness.

RULE XXV

Purpose-driven Meetings

If you have been selected to facilitate a meeting, you need to remember a few things. First, you need to develop a very clear agenda with engaging topics, subject matter experts, and time slots. Secondly, you need to consider the following questions: (1) What is the primary purpose of the meeting? (2) Are the right people included in the meeting? (3) What is the group going to accomplish by the end of the meeting? If any of these questions go unanswered, you are at risk of having a very unsuccessful meeting, which could be a blow to your credibility as a leader. **(See sample meeting agenda in the appendix section.)**

RULE XXVI

Solve the Tough Problems

At some point in your career, you are going to be asked to make very difficult decisions (e.g. layoffs, consolidating positions, closure of service lines/departments or facilities, etc.). Do not shy away from these situations! Instead, you should consider such situations as an opportunity to demonstrate fortitude and grit as a leader. As you become more comfortable with making difficult decisions, your reputation will proceed you. You can expect both recognition and promotions to follow.

RULE XXVII

Use "Other Duties as Assigned" to Your Professional Advantage

Every leadership position has a section called "other duties as assigned" included in the job description. Believe it or not, this is an opportunity for you to take on projects that you find intriguing and vital to your professional development. As you master the essential aspects of your role, stay alert of key projects or emerging opportunities to get involved and notify your supervisor immediately. After all, professional superstardom does not just appear out of thin air. You must make it happen!

RULE XXVIII

Embrace Your Mistakes

This rule will seem elementary, but its impact is profound. When people make mistakes, they usually try to hide them due to fear of retaliation or retribution. This is not an act of continuous improvement. Here's a better alternative. If you make a mistake, do not hide it. Instead, own your mistake, fix it, and move on. It is important to know why the mistake occurred and solve for the root cause as well. This approach demonstrates continuous learning and commitment to professional growth and development. As we know, leaders who do not learn do not grow and eventually become stagnant. And in this age of constant change, stagnation is not an option.

RULE XXIX

Over-appreciate Your Executive/ Administrative Assistants

In the field of leadership, executive or administrative assistants play a significant role in your success. Often times, they assist with managing calendars, coordinating meetings, proofreading reports (checking for typos), and organizing departmental events, to name a few. As you know, submitting reports with errors can be damaging to your credibility and career as a leader. To prevent such embarrassments, you need to build relationships with your assistants based on mutual respect and trust. Your assistant's goals should be connected to your goals. If you win, he/she wins. The same concept applies to failures. Applying a slogan of the *Three Musketeers*, "All for one and one for all!"

RULE XXX

Encourage Solutions

As leaders, we like to solve problems. In truth, this is what we are paid to do. However, when you manage leaders (e.g. managers, directors, vice presidents, etc.), you need to approach problem-solving differently. As leaders, our job is to set direction, listen, coach, support, cheerlead, and, of course, correct as needed. When our employees approach us with problems, many of us spring into solution mode. Please resist this temptation! Instead, you should listen to your employee, clarify the issue/problem and inquire about their solutions. The intent behind this approach is to enhance your employee's critical-thinking abilities by engaging him/her in solution development. You want the solution to come from them, not you. After all, as leaders, we are in the solutions business, not problem identification business.

CLOSING REMARKS

This book provides readers with practical tips on how to navigate the job-searching process and keeping the job once you land it. The tips shared in this book are based on actual experiences that either led to job offers or on-the-job success. The intent of this book is not to be the "end all be all." Instead, I took a stab at pulling back the curtains and demystifying professional life matters that many of us struggle with. I hope these tips bring success to readers for many years to come. As an author, I recognize that there is more to a successful career than what I have shared in this book. To this end, I welcome other authors to join me in laying out a pathway for early, mid, and senior careerists to navigate their professional journeys with more confidence and direction. In the end, leaders are called to serve others. Through this service, others are encouraged to follow those who serve them. I, as a servant leader, wish readers the best of professional success and welcome any feedback you may have about the book. Given that this is my first major published material, I count on you to help me become more effective at advancing the field of leadership.

SECTION 3

Appendices

1. Sample thank-you note
2. Sample counteroffer letter
3. Sample meeting agenda

APPENDIX 1

Sample Thank-You Note

Step 1. Purchase a high quality thank-you card. Crane & Co. is highly recommended.

Step 2. Review the notes that you captured during the interview.

Step 3. Open each thank-you card and write (do not type!) a very brief, yet customized thank-you note to each interviewer. Consider using the sample language and format below.

> **Dear (First name goes here) MM/DD/YY**
>
> **Thank you for taking the time to meet with me today. I was glad to learn more about the current state of financial affairs within Incredible Health System (IHS). I am even more interested in the Senior Vice President of Strategy opportunity and would very much like to work with you to transform IHS's financial performance and overall market position.**
>
> **Sincerely,**
> **(Signature goes here)**
> **Jane Doe, MBA**

Step 4. Place a stamp on each of your thank-you cards and send them via postal service. If you prefer that your interviewers receive thank-you cards the next day, stop by the local post office and purchase the overnight "express delivery" option.

APPENDIX 2

Sample Counteroffer Letter

JANE DOE, MBA
1234 Executive Drive
Little Rock, AR 00000
(111) 222-3333
janedoe@fictionemail.com

January 22, 2018
Mr. Hospital Leader
Chief People Officer
Incredible Health System
808 Snare Avenue
Great City, CA 99999
Re: Offer Letter

Dear Mr. Leader:

First and foremost, thank you for extending an offer on Tuesday, January 16, 2018, for the Senior Vice President of Strategy position of Incredible Health System (IHS). I am very grateful for this opportunity, excited about the offer and interested in joining the Executive Team. After taking some time to review the offer, I would like to share my thoughts regarding the details in the letter.

COMPENSATION:

In the "Compensation" section of the offer, a base salary of $325,000 was presented. During our phone interview on October 12th, we discussed the Senior Vice President position at length, my leadership experiences and base salary expectations. As noted in my records of the phone interview, before agreeing to move forward in the process and at your request, I shared a salary range of $335,000 to $415,000 with an expectation of placement between the 50th and 75th percentile. During my subsequent meetings with the Executive Team, I learned about the many exciting challenges facing your organization and believe that my contribution would be valuable to the leadership team's efforts. I would ask that your base salary offer be revised to meet the minimum level that I shared in our initial discussion on October 12, 2017.

TEMPORARY HOUSING:

According to this section of the offer, IHS will pay for temporary housing beginning upon my hiring date. However, the offer does not define "temporary housing" in any level of specificity. I seek additional clarification on temporary housing. Secondly, are utilities included in temporary housing coverage?

RELOCATION:

The offer states that IHS agrees to reimburse me for my relocation expenses from Arkansas to Great City. After thorough review and consideration, I would like for IHS to pay for my relocation from Arkansas to Great City upon my hiring date. I would also ask for IHS to furnish a copy of the relocation package for my review and understanding.

EMPLOYMENT CONTINGENCY:

The offer states that if I leave IHS within 2 years, I will be required to pay back temporary housing and relocation cost. While I have every intention of advancing the mission and vision of IHS over the long-term, if an unforeseen situation necessitates my earlier separation from IHS, I would like you to consider doing this on a "pro rata" basis (e.g. Leave after one year of service; pay back 50%, etc.) or waive this provision entirely, which is a very fair and reasonable approach.

NON-COMPETE/NON-SOLICITATION:

The offer specifies a non-compete for 24 months. This provision extends beyond severance pay of 12 months. The industry norm for non-compete is 12 months. For an executive who is relocating to Great City from a different state, I would like you to either reconsider the current non-compete provision and revise it to reflect a 12 months period, which I have found to be in alignment with industry standards for executives.

PROFESSIONAL MEMBERSHIPS:

As a health-care professional and leader, I am very much committed to continuous learning and improvement. To this end, I would like you to consider covering annual cost of memberships and conferences for my participation with the following professional associations:

- ➢ American College of Management
- ➢ Association of Strategy Professionals

BENEFITS:

In reviewing the executive benefits package, I am quite pleased with IHS's offerings. I would only ask that the waiting period, if applicable, for these benefits be waived.

OTHER NON-SALARY BENEFITS:

In addition to the aforementioned, I would also like to discuss the following options with you to ensure that my professional and personal success in the Great City area:

- Executive Coach
- Financial Planner/Analyst
- Legal Services
- Assistance with Student Loans

Once again, I am excited about the offer and opportunity to join the IHS team. Thank you for giving attention to my thoughts and considerations. I look forward to hearing from you.

Sincerely,
Jane Doe, MBA

APPENDIX 3

Sample Meeting Agenda

Department Meeting
Date: September 25, 2018
Time: 8:00 AM–12:00 PM
Organizer/Facilitator: (Enter name here)
Participants: (Enter names here)

Time	Agenda Item	Presenter	Action Required
8:00 AM	Welcome	Facilitator	
8:05 AM	Introductions	Group	
8:15 AM	Purpose of the meeting		Provide overview and goal of the meeting.
8:30 AM	Topic A—Burning Platform	Facilitator	Present burning platform and data that supports the issue discussed.
8:45 AM	Group Discussion	Group	Group reflects on burning platform and data.
9:00 AM	Brainstorming	Facilitator	A facilitated brainstorming session to develop solutions for the issue at hand.

10:00 AM	Break		
10:15 AM	Discussion and Prioritization	Facilitator	A facilitated group discussion to review and prioritize ideas for action planning purposes.
11:00 AM	Break		
11:15 AM	Next Steps	Facilitator	Provide recap the meeting and clarify next steps on the process.
11:30 AM	Q and A	Group	
11:55 AM	Next Meeting Reminder	Facilitator	Announce the date, time, and location of the next meeting.
12:00 PM	Adjournment		

ABOUT THE AUTHOR

Kris M. Drake, FACHE, is founder and president of Drake Strategic Services LLC, a management consulting firm specializing in business planning, governance, and physician alignment. Drake has been featured in the *Journal of Healthcare Management* and *ACHE* newsletter. He is a recipient of the ACHE Regent Award and a graduate of the ACHE Executive Program. Drake earned his MHA from Grand Valley State University. He is a member of the Great Lakes ACHE Board of Directors and lives in Michigan.

CPSIA information can be obtained
at www.ICGtesting.com
Printed in the USA
LVHW092110210720
661195LV00007B/677